# I CAN READ ABOUT

# FOSSILS

Written by John Howard
Illustrated by Norman Nodel

**Troll Associates**

Millions and millions of years ago, giant reptiles called dinosaurs ruled the earth. The earth was very different then. The air was warm, and the land was low and swampy.

DIPLODOCUS

The swamps were filled with plant-eating
dinosaurs like Brachiosaurus (BRAK-ee-uh-sawr-us)
and Trachodon (TRAK-uh-don).

CYCADS

BRACHIOSAURUS

TRACHODON

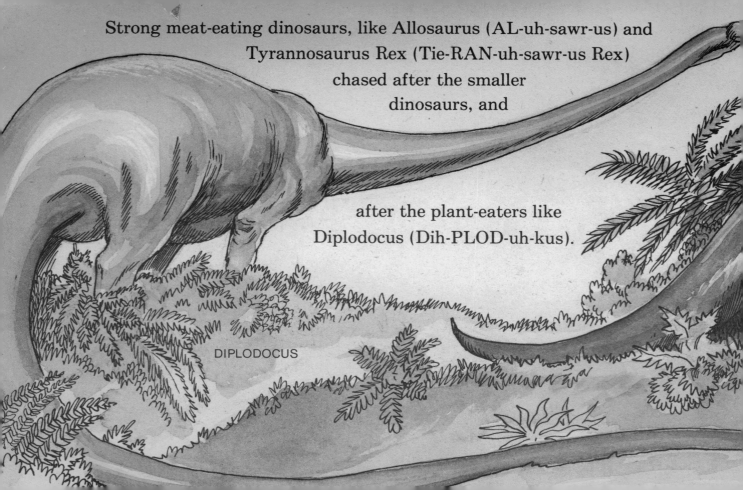

Strong meat-eating dinosaurs, like Allosaurus (AL-uh-sawr-us) and Tyrannosaurus Rex (Tie-RAN-uh-sawr-us Rex) chased after the smaller dinosaurs, and

after the plant-eaters like Diplodocus (Dih-PLOD-uh-kus).

DIPLODOCUS

The ground shook when
Tyrannosaurus Rex fought the
three-horned monster Triceratops
(Tri-SER-uh-tops).

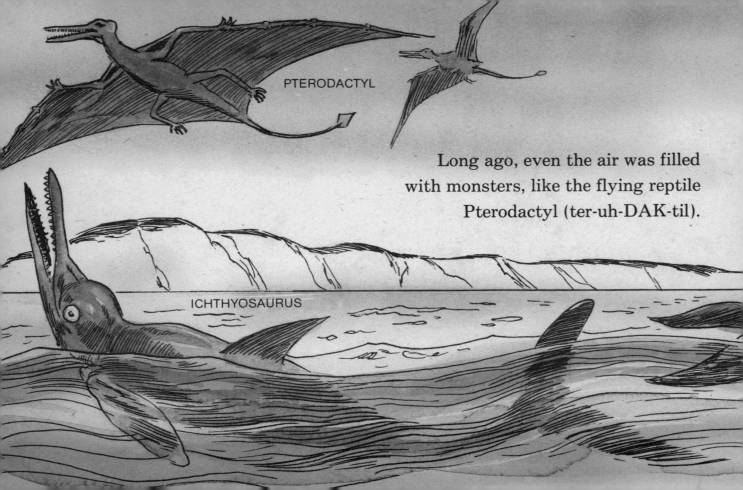

PTERODACTYL

Long ago, even the air was filled
with monsters, like the flying reptile
Pterodactyl (ter-uh-DAK-til).

ICHTHYOSAURUS

And in the sea, there were strange-looking fish
and sea serpents with razor-sharp teeth.

PLESIOSAURUS

The word dinosaur means "terrible lizard." For over 100 million years, these giant creatures ruled the earth. Then they mysteriously disappeared. Why did they die?

Some scientists think that the earth grew too cold
for the dinosaurs. They could not adapt, or change, to
the changing climate. Other scientists think that the
dinosaurs may have died off when small mammals
ate the dinosaurs' eggs.

There are no dinosaurs living on earth today.
No one has ever seen a dinosaur. But we still
know a lot about them. We know what they
looked like, what they ate, and where
some of them lived.

The dinosaurs left clues that tell us a great deal.
These clues are called fossils. Fossils are bones, teeth, footprints,
and impressions of animals and plants that lived long ago.

Fossils are usually found in sedimentary (sed-uh-MEN-tuh-ree) rocks.
Sedimentary rocks are rocks like sandstone, shale, and limestone.
They are formed when mud, sand, clay, and minerals pile up in layers.
These layers are pressed together for millions of years and turn to stone.

SANDSTONE

SHALE

LIMESTONE

When the dinosaurs died, many of them sank to the bottom of the swamps. In time, all that was left were their bones. The bones were covered with layers of mud and sand that later turned to rock.

A paleontologist (pale-ee-on-TOL-uh-just) is a scientist who studies fossils. Paleontologists are like detectives. They follow the clues and try to solve the mystery of the dinosaurs. They try to solve the mysteries of the past.

Knowing where to look is important. But even when scientists know *where* to look, fossils are not always easy to find. It can take days, months, and even years of digging to find even the smallest fossils.

A fossil hunter must carefully remove layers of rock. A small bone might be found right away. That bone is carefully wrapped to protect it. Then the search continues—one bone means that others might be hidden nearby.

Sometimes, if fossil hunters are lucky, they find entire skeletons. But most of the time, they find only small pieces, which must be put together like the pieces of a giant jigsaw puzzle.

Scientists are not the only people who find fossils. Almost 200 years ago, in England, a 12-year-old girl found something very strange. It was a complete skeleton of a 7-foot-long monster trapped in rock. It looked as if it were part fish and part lizard. Scientists decided to call it Ichthyosaurus (Ik-thee-uh-SAWR-us), which means "fish lizard."

Today we have a good idea
how Ichthyosaurus looked.

PLESIOSAURUS

The same girl later discovered two other fossil skeletons.
One was a sea serpent called Plesiosaurus (PLEE-see-uh-SAWR-us).
The other was a flying reptile called a Pterosaur (TER-uh-sawr).

Fossils of other flying reptiles have been found in Texas and Kansas. Buried in the rock were several skeletons of prehistoric, bird-like reptiles. The wings were nearly 30 feet wide.

In Montana and Wyoming, scientists found enough bones to put together two full skeletons of Tyrannosaurus Rex. Tyrannosaurus was 20 feet tall and 50 feet long.

Most of the time, fossils are not found as complete skeletons. But if enough bones are found, scientists can fill in the missing parts with plaster bones. Then, they can put the skeleton back together again.

One of the most exciting fossil treasures was found in the Gobi Desert in Mongolia. Nestled among sandstone rocks was an entire nest of dinosaur eggs.

FLAMING CLIFFS
GOBI DESERT

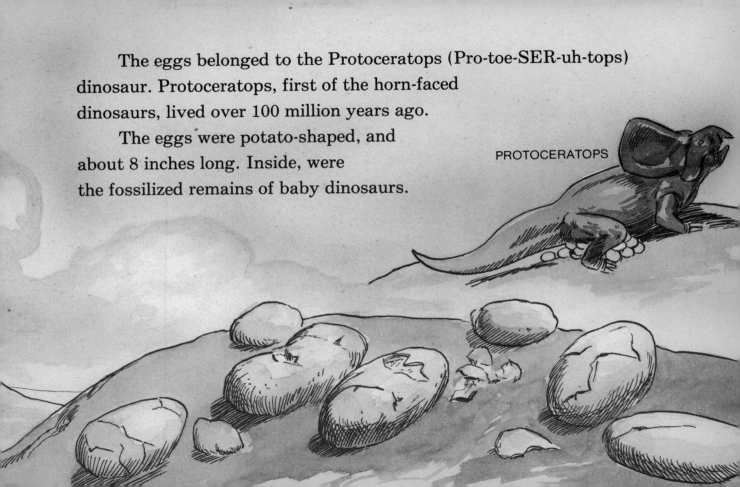

The eggs belonged to the Protoceratops (Pro-toe-SER-uh-tops) dinosaur. Protoceratops, first of the horn-faced dinosaurs, lived over 100 million years ago.

The eggs were potato-shaped, and about 8 inches long. Inside, were the fossilized remains of baby dinosaurs.

PROTOCERATOPS

MAMMOTH

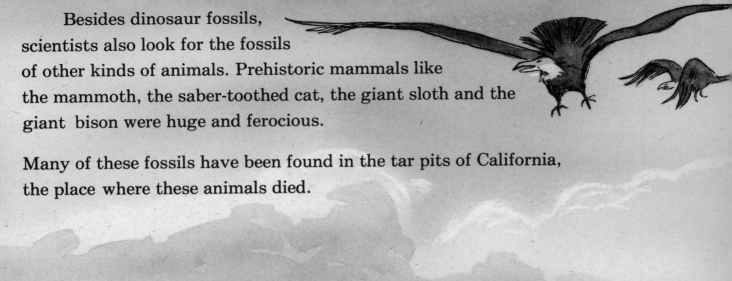

Besides dinosaur fossils, scientists also look for the fossils of other kinds of animals. Prehistoric mammals like the mammoth, the saber-toothed cat, the giant sloth and the giant bison were huge and ferocious.

Many of these fossils have been found in the tar pits of California, the place where these animals died.

Scientists think that shallow water covered the tops of the tar pits in prehistoric times. When the animals came to drink, they stepped into the water and were trapped by the sticky tar. Unable to escape, they died there and the tar fossilized their skeletons.

Over 1,000 saber-toothed skulls, and many bones, tusks, and teeth have been pulled out of the tar pits.

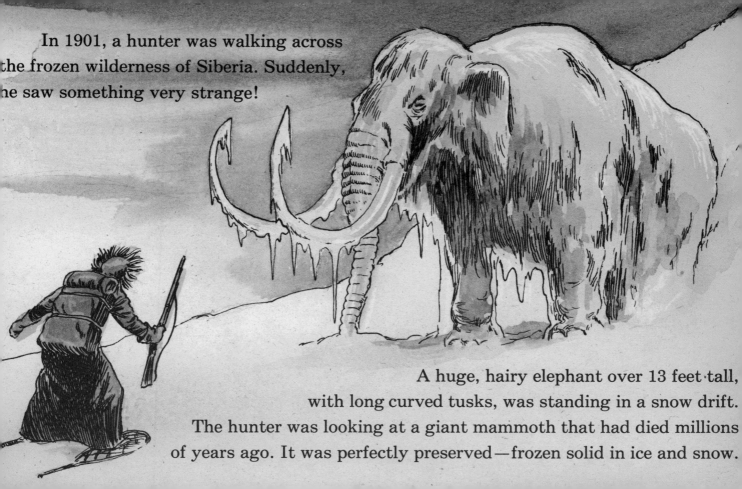

In 1901, a hunter was walking across the frozen wilderness of Siberia. Suddenly, he saw something very strange!

A huge, hairy elephant over 13 feet tall, with long curved tusks, was standing in a snow drift. The hunter was looking at a giant mammoth that had died millions of years ago. It was perfectly preserved—frozen solid in ice and snow.

Other types of fossils are impressions of plants and small animals found in rocks or coal. Sometimes, scientists find insects in amber. The insects were trapped in sticky tree sap. When the sap hardened and turned to amber rock, the insects were perfectly preserved.

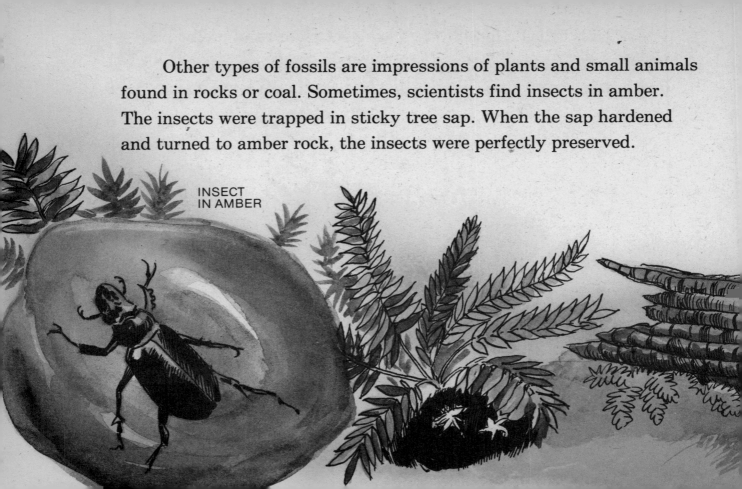

INSECT IN AMBER

Coal is called a fossil fuel. As ancient plants and prehistoric forests sank into the earth, they hardened into layers, and fossilized. The heat and pressure of the earth changed these plants and trees into coal. Fossil imprints of small animals are often found in coal formed hundreds of millions of years ago.

COAL

CONIFER TWIG

LEAF OF GINKGO TREE

JURASSIC CYCAD

SEED

Fossil impressions can tell us what life was like. They show the shapes of plants that lived millions of years ago. By studying plant life, scientists can also tell what the climate was like then.

PLANT-EATER TEETH

Every fossil, no matter how small, is important. By studying the size and shape of fossil teeth, for example, we can tell if the animal was a meat-eater or a plant-eater.

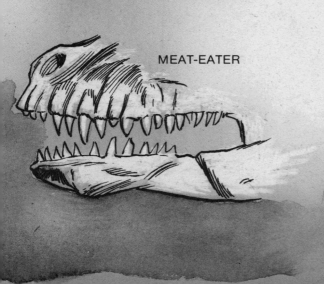

MEAT-EATER

SABER TOOTH

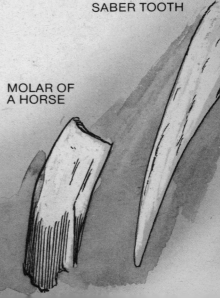

MOLAR OF A HORSE

MOLAR OF A PIG

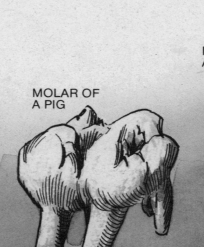

When fossils of sea creatures or fossil shells are found on dry land, scientists know that the dry land was probably covered with water in prehistoric times. Shells often give us clues to the past.

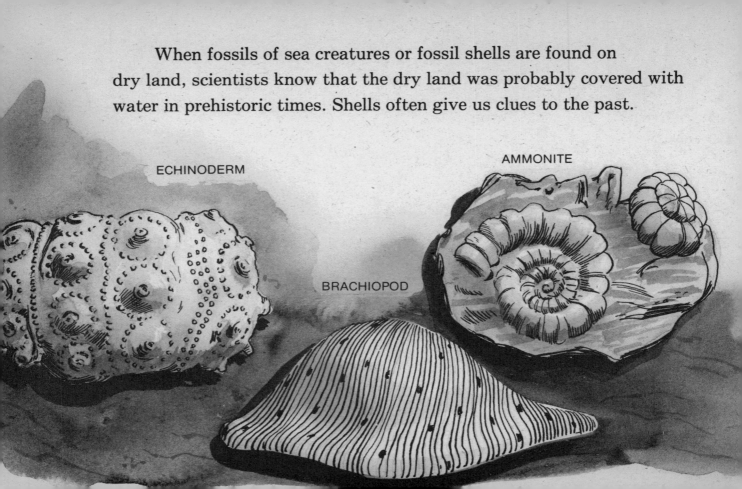

ECHINODERM

AMMONITE

BRACHIOPOD

How do you measure time?

One way is by measuring the amount of carbon found in fossils, and by studying the layers of rock where fossils are found.

SNAIL

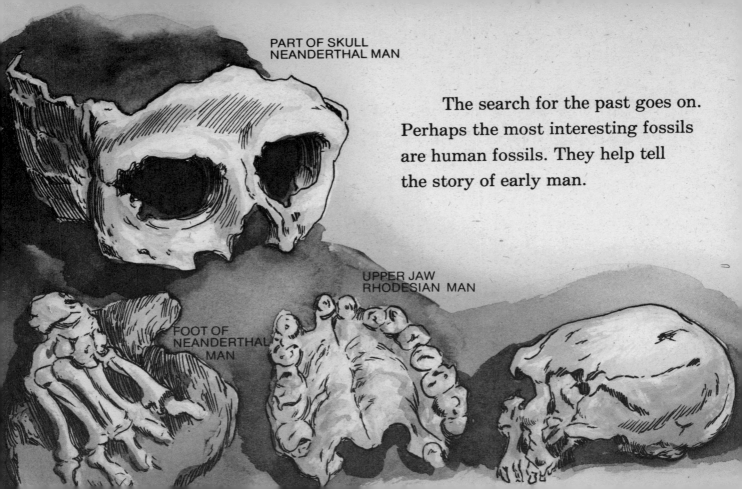

PART OF SKULL
NEANDERTHAL MAN

The search for the past goes on.
Perhaps the most interesting fossils
are human fossils. They help tell
the story of early man.

UPPER JAW
RHODESIAN MAN

FOOT OF
NEANDERTHAL
MAN

What did early people look like?
Did they use tools? Did they know how to use fire?
Fossils help tell the story, and give us clues
to the past.

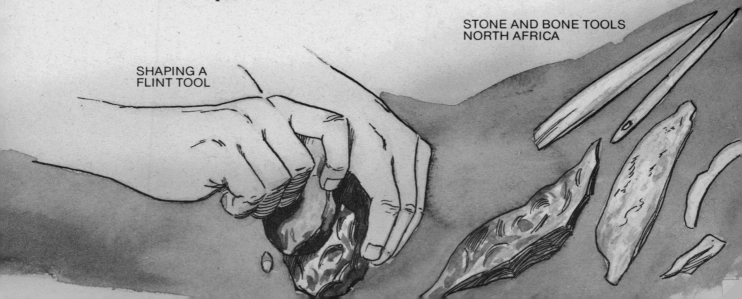

SHAPING A
FLINT TOOL

STONE AND BONE TOOLS
NORTH AFRICA

New fossils are being found all the time.
They continue to add to the story of the earth, but
there is still so much to learn.

Did other giant creatures roam the earth? What really happened to the dinosaurs and other prehistoric animals? What were early people like?

Someday we hope to learn the answers to these questions. Fossils will give us the clues and help show the way. What treasures will we find on the path to discovery?